TAKE TIME

Compiled by Dan Zadra & Kristel Wills
Designed by Sarah Forster & Jessica Phoenix
Created by Kobi Yamada

COMPENDIUM™
INCORPORATED

live inspired.

ACKNOWLEDGEMENTS

These quotations were gathered lovingly but unscientifically over several years and/or were contributed by many friends or acquaintances. Some arrived—and survived in our files—on scraps of paper and may therefore be imperfectly worded or attributed. To the authors, contributors and original sources, our thanks, and where appropriate, our apologies. –The Editors

WITH SPECIAL THANKS TO

Jason Aldrich, Gloria Austin, Gerry Baird, Jay Baird, Neil Beaton, Josie Bissett, Laura Boro, Chris Dalke, Jim and Alyssa Darragh & Family, Tom DesLongchamp, Jennifer and Matt Ellison & Family, Rob Estes, Michael and Leianne Flynn & Family, Jennifer Hurwitz, Heidi Jones, Carol Anne Kennedy, June Martin, Steve and Janet Potter & Family, Diane Roger, Kirsten and Garrett Sessions, Clarie Yam and Erik Lee, Heidi Yamada & Family, Justi and Tote Yamada & Family, Bob and Val Yamada, Kaz and Kristin Yamada & Family, Tai and Joy Yamada, Anne Zadra, August and Arline Zadra, and Gus and Rosie Zadra.

CREDITS

Compiled by Dan Zadra & Kristel Wills
Designed by Sarah Forster & Jessica Phoenix
Created by Kobi Yamada

ISBN: 978-1-932319-60-6

1st Printing. 7500 02 08   Printed in China

THERE COMES A TIME WHEN YOU PUT YOURSELF AT THE TOP OF YOUR COMMITMENT LIST.

Marian Wright Edelman

Life moves pretty quickly these days. We make time for work and other obligations, and that's important. But life is not just an obligation, it's an adventure.

Whatever happened to simple pleasures and spontaneous experiences? Where are the little interludes in your day for loving, laughing, loafing or learning? At what point did you lose the right to do something wonderful for yourself—not because you have to, but because you want to?

This is your life, and you don't want to miss it. Possibilities for adventure, beauty, relaxation and contribution are all around you—and you really can make time for them. As Liane Steele once wrote, "Be assured that you will always find time for the things you put first." Happiness is always in your hands.

TAKE TIME TO PLAN.

How are you going to use
your supply of tomorrows?

Kobi Yamada

TAKE TIME TO REFLECT.

Whatever you do in this life,
take time to sit quietly and let
the world tell you what it needs
from you. Take a moment to
honestly understand what your
gifts are—you have them.

Ann Reed

TAKE TIME TO BE YOURSELF.

Embrace your uniqueness.
Time is much too short to be
living someone else's life.

Unknown

TAKE TIME TO MAKE A DIFFERENCE.

There are many wonderful
things that will never be done
if you do not do them.

Charles D. Gill

TAKE TIME TO PRIORITIZE.

The minute you begin to do
what you really want to do,
it's really a different kind of life.

R. Buckminster Fuller

TAKE TIME TO IMAGINE.

Let your mind fly toward "what-if?"
Let your what-if become "why-not?"
Then you're on your way.

Earnie Larsen and Carole Larsen

TAKE TIME TO BE CREATIVE.

Make something every day.
Make a song, make a move, make
a friend, make a difference.

Pat Collelo

TAKE TIME TO LET GO.

Do yourself a favor.
Overlook at least two things today.

M.J. Ryan

TAKE TIME TO FOLLOW THROUGH.

Turn the wheel of your life. Make complete revolutions. Celebrate every turning. And persevere with joy.

Deng Ming-Dao

TAKE TIME TO BALANCE YOUR LIFE.

Learn some and think some and draw
and paint and sing and dance and
play and work every day some.

Robert Fulghum

TAKE TIME TO UNWIND.

At times, each of us needs to
withdraw from the cares which
will not withdraw from us.

Maya Angelou

TAKE TIME TO BE ALONE.

In solitude we give passionate
attention to our lives, to our memories,
to the details around us.

Virginia Woolf

TAKE TIME TO DO NOTHING.

Rest is not idleness, and to
lie sometimes on the grass under
the trees on a summer's day, listening
to the murmur of water, or watching
the clouds float across the sky is by
no means a waste of time.

J. Lubbock

TAKE TIME FOR INTUITION.

Your heart often knows things
before your mind does.

Polly Adler

TAKE TIME FOR YOUR SPIRIT.

Just put your ear down next
to your soul and listen hard.

Anne Sexton

TAKE TIME FOR WELLNESS.

If you don't make time to take
care of yourself, who will?

Connie Podesta

TAKE TIME TO PLAY.

Never lose your child's heart.

Mencius

TAKE TIME FOR LAUGHTER.

Laugh often, long and loud. Laugh until you gasp for breath. And if you have a friend who makes you laugh, spend lots and lots of time with them.

Unknown

TAKE TIME TO BE FREE.

Guard well your spare moments. They are like uncut diamonds. Discard them and their value will never be known. Improve them and they will become the brightest gems in a useful life.

Ralph Waldo Emerson

TAKE TIME TO EXPLORE.

Every once in awhile, take the scenic route.

H. Jackson Brown, Jr.

TAKE TIME TO SEE THE GOOD.

One hour devoted to the pursuit
of beauty and love is worth
a full century of glory.

Kahlil Gibran

TAKE TIME TO MARVEL.

The moment one gives close
attention to anything, even a blade
of grass, it becomes a mysterious,
awesome, indescribably magnificent
world in itself.

Henry Miller

TAKE TIME FOR SPONTANEITY.

We get so busy making a living that we forget to live. At what point did you lose the right to do something in your day just because you feel like it at the moment—just because you're alive?

Dan Zadra

TAKE TIME FOR THE HERE AND NOW.

Whatever I'm doing at the moment
is the biggest thing in life—whether
it is conducting a symphony
or peeling an orange.

Arturo Toscanini

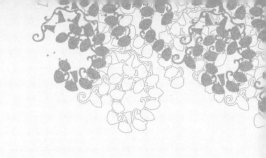

TAKE TIME FOR ART AND BEAUTY.

Art washes away from the soul
the dust of everyday life.

Pablo Picasso

TAKE TIME TO BE KIND.

Person to person, moment to moment,
as we love, we change the world.

Samahria Lyte Kaufman

TAKE TIME TO DARE.

If you keep following your own footprints,
you will end up where you began, but
if you stretch yourself you will flourish.

Donna Basplay

TAKE TIME TO MAKE THE WORLD BETTER

Go out and make a difference in your community. You don't need endless time and perfect conditions. Do it now. Do it today. Do it for twenty minutes and watch your heart start beating.

Barbara Sher

TAKE TIME TO CELEBRATE OTHERS.

We all need to be recognized for what we're doing, for our work. Every once in a while we need someone to come up to us and say, "You're beautiful. That was well done. That's nice."

Leo Buscaglia

TAKE TIME TO RECONNECT.

Certain people have meant the world to you at one time or another. Today, a handwritten card or call from you—out of the blue—would mean the world to them.

Dan Zadra

TAKE TIME TO MEET NEW PEOPLE.

Your life can be changed in a matter of hours by people who don't even know you yet.

Unknown

TAKE TIME FOR ROMANCE.

The flower, the sky, your beloved can only be found in the present moment.

Thich Nhat Hanh

TAKE TIME FOR LOVE.

Live simply; love lavishly.

Michael Nolan

TAKE TIME FOR FRIENDSHIP.

A friend is one of the nicest
things you can have, and one
of the best things you can be.

Douglas Pagels

TAKE TIME FOR FAMILY.

Treasure each other in the recognition
that we do not know how long
we shall have each other.

Joshua Loth Liebman

TAKE TIME FOR REFRESHMENT.

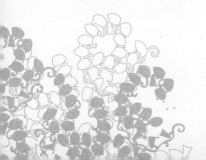

Over and over, we have to go back to the beginning. We should not be ashamed of this. It is good. It's like drinking water.

Natalie Goldberg

TAKE TIME FOR NEW POSSIBILITIES.

Allow yourself the freedom to grow and expand. Form the habit of saying yes to your own potential. Take time to think of all the reasons why you can and will embrace wondrous new possibilities and adventures.

Don Ward

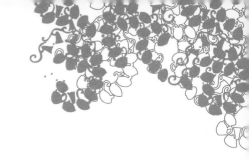

TAKE TIME FOR GRATITUDE.

This is the gift—to have the wonderful
capacity to appreciate again and again,
freshly and naively, the basic goods
of life, with awe, pleasure, wonder,
and even ecstasy.

Abraham Maslow

How we spend our days is, of course,
how we spend our lives.

Annie Dillard